Stems

by Gail Saunders-Smith

Photo: Tulip Stems

Content Consultant:
Deborah Brown, Horticulturist
University of Minnesota Extension Service

an imprint of Capstone Press

Pebble Books are published by Capstone Press
818 North Willow Street, Mankato, Minnesota 56001
http://www.capstone-press.com

Library of Congress Cataloging in Publication Data
Saunders-Smith, Gail.
    Stems/by Gail Saunders-Smith
        p. cm.
    Includes bibliographical references (p. 23) and index.
    Summary: Describes the different kinds of roots and stems flowers may have and their
importance in helping flowers to grow.
    ISBN 1-56065-772-3
    1. Stems (Botany)--Juvenile literature. 2. Roots (Botany)--Juvenile literature. [1. Flowers. 2.
Stems (Botany) 3. Roots (Botany)] I. Title.
    QK646.S3 1998
    575.4--dc21   98-5047
                                                                          CIP
                                                                          AC

Note to Parents and Teachers

This book describes and illustrates how a flower uses roots and stems. The close
picture-text matches support early readers in understanding the text. The text
offers subtle challenges with compound and complex sentence structures. This
book also introduces early readers to expository and content-specific
vocabulary. The expository vocabulary is defined in the Words to Know section.
Early readers may need assistance in reading some of these words. Readers also
may need assistance in using the Table of Contents, Words to Know, Read More,
Internet Sites and Index/Word List sections of the book.

2

Table of Contents

4

Flowers need roots and stems. Roots grow away from light. They grow into the soil. Roots take in water and food from the soil.

Roots also help flowers stand. They hold plants in the ground. Then water and wind cannot move the plants.

Some flowers have fibrous roots. Fibrous roots are thin. They spread out in the ground. They usually do not grow very deep into the ground.

Photo: Marigold

Other flowers have tap roots. A tap root is thick and grows straight down. Tap roots may grow deep into the ground. Some smaller roots grow out from the tap root.

Stems connect to the roots. Stems grow above the ground. Leaves grow on the sides of stems. Flower buds grow at the tips of stems. Stems can carry one flower or many flowers.

Stems carry water and food. They get water and food from the roots. Water and food travel up the stems to the leaves and flowers.

Stems also carry food from the leaves. The leaves make food from sunlight. The stems carry this food to the rest of the plant.

18

Some stems are thick and stiff. Others are thin and bendable. Some stems are smooth. Some have thorns. Thorns may keep animals from eating a plant.

Photo: Rose Stem

20

Some stems grow straight up. Others grow along the ground. Some stems climb. They grow up the sides of buildings or wrap around other plants.

Words to Know

fibrous root—a kind of root with thin parts that look like strings; fibrous roots spread out in the ground.

smooth—without bumps

soil—dirt or earth; plants grow in soil.

tap root—a kind of root with a long, thick part that goes deep into the ground

thorn—a sharp point that grows from a stem

Read More

Bryant-Mole, Karen. *Flowers.* See for Yourself. Austin, Texas: Raintree Steck-Vaughn, 1996.

Butler, Daphne. *What Happens when Flowers Grow.* Austin, Texas: Raintree Steck-Vaughn, 1995.

Rowe, Julian. *Watch It Grow!* First Science. Chicago: Children's Press, 1994.

Internet Sites

4-H Children's Garden
http://commtechlab.msu.edu/sites/garden/index.html

Kids' World: Virgil Life Science Activities
http://www.kidsworld.com/kidsworld/virgil/activity/life/vwexp003.htm

Plants
http://www.ed.gov/pubs/parents/Science/plants.html

Welcome to the Flowerbase
http://www.flowerbase.com

Index/Word List

animals, 19
buds, 13
buildings, 21
fibrous roots, 9
flowers, 5, 7, 9, 11, 13, 15
food, 5, 15, 17
ground, 7, 9, 11, 13, 21
leaves, 13, 15, 17
light, 5

plant, 7, 17, 19, 21
roots, 5, 7, 9, 11, 13, 15
soil, 5
stems, 5, 13, 15, 17, 19, 21
sunlight, 17
tap root, 11
thorns, 19
water, 5, 7, 15
wind, 7

Word Count: 232
Early-Intervention Level: 10

Editorial Credits
Lois Wallentine, editor; James Franklin, designer; Michelle L. Norstad, photo researcher

Photo Credits
Chuck Place, cover
Dan Suzio, 12, 20
Dwight Kuhn, 4, 8, 10, 18
KAC Productions/Kathy Adams Clark, 16
Richard Hamilton Smith, 1
Unicorn Stock Photos/Dennis Thompson, 6
William Muñoz, 14

575,4
SAU

10/00